BARACK OBAMA
of THEE I SING

A Letter to My Daughters

ILLUSTRATED BY LOREN LONG

BARACK OBAMA

of THEE I SING

A Letter to My Daughters

ILLUSTRATED BY LOREN LONG

PUFFIN

To Michelle — whose fierce love and daily good sense
have nourished such wonderful daughters
—B.O.

To my sons, Griff and Graham
—L.L.

PUFFIN BOOKS

UK | USA | Canada | Ireland | Australia
India | New Zealand | South Africa

Puffin Books is part of the Penguin Random House group of companies
whose addresses can be found at global.penguinrandomhouse.com.

www.penguin.co.uk   www.puffin.co.uk   www.ladybird.co.uk

 Penguin
Random House
UK

First published in the USA by Alfred A. Knopf 2010
This edition published in Great Britain by Puffin Books 2018

001

Text copyright © Barack Obama, 2010
Cover art and illustrations copyright © Loren Long, 2010
The moral right of the author and illustrator has been asserted

The text of this book is set in Cochin
The illustrations were created using acrylic on board

Printed in China
A CIP catalogue record for this book is available from the British Library

ISBN: 978–0–241–37090–2

All correspondence to:
Puffin Books, Penguin Random House Children's
80 Strand, London WC2R 0RL

MIX
Paper from
responsible sources
FSC® C018179

Have I told you lately how wonderful you are?
How the sound of your feet
running from afar
brings dancing rhythms to my day?
How you laugh
and sunshine spills into the room?

Have I told you

that you are creative?

A woman named Georgia O'Keeffe
moved to the desert and painted petals, bone, bark.
She helped us see big beauty in what is small:
the hardness of stone and the softness of feather.

Have I told you that you are smart?

That you braid great ideas with imagination?
A man named Albert Einstein
turned pictures in his mind into giant advances in science,
changing the world
with energy and light.

Have I told you that you are brave?

A man named Jackie Robinson played baseball

and showed us all

how to turn fear to respect

and respect to love.

He swung his bat with the grace and strength of a lion

and gave brave dreams to other dreamers.

Have I told you that you are a healer?

Sitting Bull was a Sioux medicine man
who healed broken hearts and broken promises.
It is fine that we are different, he said.
"For peace, it is not necessary for eagles to be crows."
Though he was put in prison,
his spirit soared free on the plains, and his wisdom
touched the generations.

Have I told you

that you have your own song?

A woman named Billie Holiday wore a gardenia in her hair
and sang beautiful blues to the world.
Her voice, full of sadness and joy,
made people feel deeply and add their melodies to the chorus.

Have I told you that you are strong?

A woman named Helen Keller fought her way through long,
silent darkness.
Though she could not see or hear,
she taught us to look at and listen to each other.
Never waiting for life to get easier,
she gave others courage to face their challenges.

Have I told you how important it is

to honor others' sacrifices?

A woman named Maya Lin designed the Vietnam Veterans Memorial
to remember those who gave their lives in the war,
and the Civil Rights Memorial
to thank the many who fought for equality.
Public spaces should be filled with art, she thought,
so that we can walk amidst it,
recalling the past and inspired to fix the future.

Have I told you that you are kind?

A woman named Jane Addams fed the poor
and helped them find jobs.
She opened doors and gave people hope.
She taught adults and invited children
to play and laugh and let their spirits grow wide.

Have I told you that you don't give up?

When violence erupted in our nation
a man named Martin Luther King Jr.
taught us unyielding compassion. He gave us a dream
that all races and creeds would walk hand in hand.
He marched and he prayed and, one at a time,
opened hearts and saw the birth of his dream in us.

Have I told you that you are an explorer?

A man named Neil Armstrong was the first to walk on the moon.

He watched the world from way up high

and we watched his lunar landing leaps,

which made us brave enough

to take our own big, bold strides.

Have I told you that you are inspiring?

A man named Cesar Chavez showed farmworkers their own power
when they felt they had none.
The people were poor but worked hard and loved the land.
Cesar picketed, prayed, and talked.
The people listened to their hearts and marched for their rights.
"¡Sí se puede!" Cesar said. "Yes, you can!"

Have I told you

that you are part of a family?

A man named Abraham Lincoln knew
that all of America should work together.
He kept our nation one
and promised freedom to enslaved sisters and brothers.
This man of the people, simple and plain,
asked more of our country—that we behave as kin.

Have I told you

to be proud to be American?

Our first president, George Washington,
believed in liberty and justice for all.
His barefoot soldiers crossed wintry rivers, forging ever on.
He helped make an idea into a new country, strong and true,
a country of principles, a country of citizens.

Have I told you that America is
made up of people of every kind?

People of all races, religions, and beliefs.
People from the coastlines and the mountains.
People who have made bright lights shine
by sharing their unique gifts
and giving us the courage to lift one another up,
to keep up the fight,
to work and build upon all that is good
in our nation.

Have I told you that they are all a part of you?
Have I told you that you are one of them,
and that you are the future?
And have I told you that I love you?

GEORGIA O'KEEFFE (1887–1986) is one of America's best-known artists. Born in Wisconsin, she also lived in New York City; near Lake George, New York; and in New Mexico, and is most famous for her exquisite large paintings of flowers and bones that she saw in the Southwest.

ALBERT EINSTEIN (1897–1955) was born in Germany, immigrated to America in 1933, and became a U.S. citizen in 1940. A recipient of the Nobel Prize, this esteemed physicist and Princeton University professor is best known for his special theory of relativity, which made famous the equation $E = mc^2$.

JACKIE ROBINSON (1919–1972) was born to a family of sharecroppers in Georgia. He excelled at athletics early on and in 1947 became the first African American to play major league baseball since the sport had become segregated in the nineteenth century. He was chosen as the National League's most valuable player in 1949.

SITTING BULL (c. 1831–1890) was a Sioux leader who spoke out and led his people against many policies of the United States government. He is most famous for his stunning victory in 1876 over Lieutenant Colonel George Armstrong Custer in the Battle of the Little Bighorn.

BILLIE HOLIDAY (1915–1959) rose from a difficult childhood to become one of the defining singers of American popular music and jazz. Holiday is known for the rich emotion in her voice. Her most famous performances include "What a Little Moonlight Can Do," "God Bless the Child," "Summertime," and "Stormy Weather."

HELEN KELLER (1880–1968) became deaf and blind as a toddler and later achieved world renown as an author and activist. She received a bachelor's degree from Radcliffe College and remained an unrelenting voice for the disabled and for many other causes throughout her life. She received the Presidential Medal of Freedom in 1964.

MAYA LIN (1959–) is an artist and architect who is best known for her design of the Vietnam Veterans Memorial in Washington, DC. She won a nationwide competition to design the memorial at the age of twenty-one, when she was an undergraduate at Yale. The memorial includes a granite wall with the names of fallen and missing soldiers. Millions of people visit the memorial every year.

JANE ADDAMS (1860–1935) was a social reformer dedicated to helping children, eradicating poverty, and promoting peace. Hull House, the settlement house she founded in Chicago, was internationally recognized in its day for its work to house the poor. Jane Addams was the second woman to receive the Nobel Peace Prize, in 1931.

DR. MARTIN LUTHER KING JR. (1929–1968) was a Baptist minister in Atlanta and an icon of the civil rights movement. His inspiring leadership of the nonviolent movement for social change, including the Montgomery Bus Boycott of 1955–56 and the March on Washington in 1963, paved the way for the desegregation of America. He received the Nobel Peace Prize in 1964.

NEIL ARMSTRONG (1930–) was an aviator and astronaut who became the first person to walk on the moon, which he did on July 20, 1969, as part of the *Apollo 11* mission. When he set foot on the lunar surface, he famously declared, "That's one small step for [a] man, one giant leap for mankind." He received the Presidential Medal of Freedom that same year, along with fellow crewmember Buzz Aldrin.

CESAR CHAVEZ (1927–1993), a farmworker since childhood, was a major leader of the nonviolent movement for the rights and dignity of farmworkers, using techniques such as strikes, boycotts, and fasts to implement social change. He cofounded the National Farm Workers Association, which became United Farm Workers, and won many crucial labor reforms. He was posthumously awarded the Presidential Medal of Freedom in 1994.

ABRAHAM LINCOLN (1809–1865) was the sixteenth president of the United States. He held office during the Civil War, which broke out on the eve of his inauguration, and he saw the nation restored to unity in 1865. In 1863 he signed the Emancipation Proclamation, freeing slaves in the Confederate states, and pressed for the passage of the Thirteenth Amendment, which abolished slavery in the United States. He was a brilliant orator whose famous speeches include the Gettysburg Address in 1863, honoring fallen soldiers of the Civil War. Lincoln was assassinated by John Wilkes Booth five days after the end of the war.

GEORGE WASHINGTON (1732–1799) was a gentleman farmer who became the commander of the Continental Army during the American Revolution, served as a delegate to and president of the Constitutional Convention, and ultimately was unanimously elected as the first president of the newly formed United States of America.

BARACK OBAMA was the forty-fourth president of the United States and the recipient of the Nobel Peace Prize in 2009. He is the author of the *New York Times* bestsellers *Dreams from My Father* and *The Audacity of Hope*. Born in Hawaii to a mother from Kansas and a father from Kenya, he himself is now the father of two daughters, Malia and Sasha. It was spending time with them that inspired him to write *Of Thee I Sing*.

LOREN LONG is the bestselling and award-winning author and illustrator of many beloved books for children, including *Drummer Boy* and the *New York Times* bestseller *Otis*. Born in Missouri and raised in Lexington, Kentucky, he is also the illustrator of Watty Piper's *The Little Engine That Could*, as well as *Toy Boat*, *I Dream of Trains*, and *Wind Flyers*. He lives in Ohio with his wife, Tracy, their two sons, Griffith and Graham, and their dogs, Elle and Moon.

In this tender, beautiful letter to his daughters, Barack Obama has written a moving tribute to thirteen groundbreaking Americans and the ideals that have shaped our nation. From the artistry of Georgia O'Keeffe to the courage of Jackie Robinson, from the strength of Helen Keller to the patriotism of George Washington, Barack Obama sees the traits of these heroes within his own children, and within all of America's children.

Stunning, evocative illustrations by award-winning artist Loren Long at once capture the personalities and achievements of these great Americans and the innocence and promise of childhood.

This beautiful book is about the potential within each of us to pursue our dreams and forge our own paths. It celebrates the characteristics that unite all Americans, from our nation's founders to the generations to come. It is a treasure to cherish with your family forever.